Grammar Success

Raising Writing Standards

Pie Corbett   Rachel Roberts

OXFORD

Great Clarendon Street, Oxford OX2 6DP

Oxford University Press is a department of the University of Oxford.
It furthers the University's objective of excellence in research, scholarship,
and education by publishing worldwide in

Oxford New York

Auckland Bangkok Buenos Aires Cape Town Chennai
Dar es Salaam Delhi Hong Kong Istanbul Karachi Kolkata
Kuala Lumpur Madrid Melbourne Mexico City Mumbai Nairobi
São Paulo Shanghai Singapore Taipei Tokyo Toronto

with an associated company in Berlin

Oxford is a registered trade mark of Oxford University Press
in the UK and in certain other countries

British Library Cataloguing in Publication Data

Data available

ISBN 0 19 834288 8

10 9 8 7 6 5 4 3 2 1

Typeset and designed by Oxford Designers and Illustrators

Printed in Hong Kong

With thanks to Ben Roberts, Ailsa McCaughrean, Greg Tremain and
Antonia Gray for the children's work feature on the cover of *Grammar
Success 4*.

Preface

Grammar Success is about teaching children how to use grammar to improve their writing. It provides materials, not only to deepen children's grammatical understanding, but also to refine their grammatical skills and to enable them to apply these to their own writing.

The course is built around the National Literacy Framework sentence level objectives. However, where there are gaps in the framework (for instance, the omission of nouns from Year 3) these have been addressed. Each unit is broken down into four sessions, based around the pupils' book, *Teacher's Guide* and the *Overhead Transparency Pack*.

Session 1 uses an OHT to introduce the grammatical objective to the children. This part of the session should be lively and interactive. Children then deepen their understanding of the particular grammatical feature through various independent activities. By the end of Session 1, pupils should be in a position to define their understanding of the objective.

Session 2 uses the pupils' book unit, plus photocopiable activities in the *Teacher's Guide*. Pupils focus upon the grammatical feature in the context of wide-ranging stimulus texts. The children are asked comprehension questions on each text before moving into activities that focus upon the grammatical feature in use. By the end of this session, pupils have critically reflected upon the use of the objective through their reading.

Session 3 relates again to the text in the pupils' book, which now becomes a model for children's own writing. The teacher's notes describe in detail how to carry out shared writing, demonstrating how to use the grammatical feature in the process of writing a new text. A photocopiable Reminder Sheet in the *Teacher's Guide* provides a summary, defining the grammatical feature and giving guidance on how to use it effectively in writing. It can be used for activities flagged by the symbol ⌶. The session ends with pupils producing their own work, drawing on the shared writing experience.

Session 4 provides an opportunity to develop writing skills, embedding the grammatical feature into the child's repertoire as a writer. This may involve revisiting and refining what was written in the third session, building upon notes or a plan already begun, or by writing a further example in the light of what was written in session 3. It is important to revisit and refine children's usage of any grammatical point so that it becomes part and parcel of their ongoing writing.

While a full range of texts and outcomes are provided in the pupils' book, children will gain greater understanding of the grammar if all three elements of the course are available to them.

Activities are differentiated in both the pupils' book (A–C) and *Teacher's Guide* to allow for pupils who may struggle or who need an extra challenge. The photocopiable activities double as a valuable homework resource.

The course helps pupils to understand grammar but also to become skilful in the key grammatical skills of:

- sentence construction
- punctuation
- enhancing writing with different language effects
- cohesion – links within and between sentences, paragraphs and texts.

The more adept children are at using these skills in their writing, the more freedom they will have to focus upon the act of creative composition.

Pie Corbett

Dear Year 6 pupils,

Year 6 marks an important stage in your education. In May, you will complete your Key Stage 2 tests and in September, most of you will transfer to secondary school. This book has been especially written to extend your experience of reading and writing in your final terms of Key Stage 2. It will help you review all the skills you have already mastered, but it will also encourage you to develop new skills as you prepare for the Key Stage 2 tests in English. You will be building your knowledge and understanding of how language works in order to improve your own writing for a range of different purposes and audiences. Not only will your learning ensure that you achieve the best possible level in your test, but you will also be laying good foundations for your future learning.

A very famous poet, Samuel Taylor Coleridge, once said that poetry was "the best words in the best order". As you study the texts in this book with your teacher, there is a good chance that you might decide that Coleridge's idea sums up many other types of writing, as well as poetry.

Good luck, and enjoy learning.

Frances Gregory

To Key Stage 2 and 3 teachers

Year 6 is a crucial point in a pupil's education. It is the year in which they sit their second major set of national tests, and for many, it is the last year of primary education. By the Summer term, Year 6 pupils should have had a wide and varied experience of reading and writing. The Key Stage 2 English tests invite them to display their knowledge, skills and understanding by asking them to engage in reading and writing texts. Teachers are advised (DfES 0135/2002) to spend time helping pupils to become more proficient readers and writers throughout Year 6 – not simply preparing for the test:

> The Literacy Hour should not be suspended in favour of continuous 'practising' for the end of Key Stage test. Rather, it should be used to teach children the compositional skills of planning, structure, sequence, sentence construction, use of appropriate language, etc and teachers should use group work for writing conferences to review, evaluate and refine work in progress.

Only a few months after the Key Stage 2 test, pupils move into Key Stage 3. Good progress will rest upon the richness of their experience of reading and writing at Key Stage 2. *Grammar Success 4* provides such richness, encouraging pupils to develop their understanding of how language works as they read and as they write.

Furthermore, with the advent of the Key Stage 3 National Strategy, Year 6 and Year 7 teachers are being supported and encouraged to work together to ensure a smoother transition between the key stages. Key Stage 2 teachers, inspired and directed by NLS *Grammar For Writing* training, have developed an expertise in developing pupil writing through close and detailed analysis of texts at sentence level. Key Stage 3 *Grammar for Writing* training is ensuring that Year 7 teachers are attuned to the vocabulary of language analysis used in Key Stage 2. A study of the sentence level teaching objectives for Year 6 and Year 7 confirms the smooth progression made possible by the Strategies. For example, the Year 6 and Year 7 objectives on complex sentences, as set out in the table on page 7, illustrate this point clearly.

Confident that terminology will be understood, both pupils and teachers can build on existing knowledge and understanding. Pupil writing will continue to develop and mature as they master the structure of the English language for a wide range of purposes.

Grammar Success 4 presents a clear programme of study for Year 6 pupils, which will not only improve their performance in tests but will also prepare them for secondary education. Year 7 teachers will find *Grammar Success 4* a useful reference point as they review their pupils' learning. In particular, it will provide appropriate support for those pupils at Key Stage 3 working below level 4. In learning how to handle the building blocks of language, pupils are gaining skills that equip and empower them for their many and varied future careers.

Frances Gregory is an ex-teacher and currently a Key Stage 3 Literacy Consultant in West Berkshire. With her Key Stage 2 colleagues, she has been researching successful transition between Key Stages 2 and 3, focusing on literacy objectives.

Year 6	Year 7
Term 1 To form complex sentences through • Using different connecting devices • Reading back complex sentences for clarity of meaning • Evaluating which links work best • Exploring how meaning is affected by the sequence and structure of clauses	Pupils should be taught to: Extend their use and control of complex sentences by: • Recognising and using subordinate clauses • Exploring the functions of subordinate clauses eg. relative clauses such as 'which I bought' or adverbial clauses such as 'having finished his' • Deploying subordinate clauses in a variety of positions within the sentence.
Term 2 To revise work on complex sentences • Identifying main clauses • Constructing complex sentences • Ways of connecting clauses • Appropriate use of punctuation	
Term 3 To secure control of complex sentences understanding how clauses can be manipulated to achieve different effects	

Sources

The texts used in this book are extracted from the following full sources, and we are grateful for their permission to reproduce copyright material.

p 10 Extract from *Milo's Wolves* by Jenny Nimmo (Egmont Children's Books, 2001), reprinted by permission of David Higham Associates.

p 12 Extract from *Holes* by Louis Sachar (Bloomsbury Children's Books, 2000), reprinted by permission of the publisher.

p 14 Extract from *Storm Catchers* by Tim Bowler (Oxford University Press, 2001), copyright © Tim Bowler 2001, reprinted by permission of David Higham Associates.

p 18 Extract adapted from *The Roman Record* by Paul Dowswell (Usborne Publishing Ltd, 83–85 Saffron Hill, London EC1N 8RT, 1997), copyright © Usborne Publishing Ltd 1997, reprinted by permission of the publisher.

p 22 Extract adapted from *Plant* by David Burnie (Dorling Kindersley, 1989), copyright © Dorling Kindersley Ltd 1989, reprinted by permission of The Penguin Group.

p 24 Extract from *Cirque du Freak* by Darren Shan (HarperCollins, 2000), reprinted by permission of the publisher.

p 36 Extract from *The War of the Worlds* by H. G. Wells (William Heinemann, 1898), reprinted by permission of A. P. Watt Ltd on behalf of the Executors of the Estate of H. G. Wells.

p 42 Extract adapted from 'Uniform Approach' by Rachel Clews, St. John Bosco Catholic High School, first publishing in Excellence in Liverpool Project's *Pressgang* magazine, Vol. 1, Issue 3, October 2000, copyright © Eclipse Publishing Ltd 2000, reprinted by permission of School Newspaper Project.

p 44 Extract from *Kensuke's Kingdom* by Michael Morpurgo (Heinemann Young Books, an imprint of Egmont Children's Books Ltd, 1999), copyright © Michael Morpurgo 1999, reprinted by permission of David Higham Associates.

p 46 Extract from 'Orpheus in the Underworld' from *The Kingfisher Book of Myths and Legends* retold by Anthony Horowitz (Kingfisher, 1985).

p 48 Text and illustrations from *Horrible Geography: Violent Volcanoes* by Anita Ganeri, illustrator Mike Phillips (Scholastic Children's Books, 1999), text copyright © Anita Ganeri 1999, illustrations copyright © Mike Phillips 1999, reprinted by permission of the publisher.

p 52 Extract adapted from *Our children, their future – A manifesto* by Barnardo's / Child Poverty Action Group / NSPCC from www.nspcc.org.uk/childrensmanifesto, reprinted by permission of National Society for the Prevention of Cruelty to Children.

p 54 Extract from *Fever Pitch* by Nick Hornby (Victor Gollancz, 1992), copyright © Nick Hornby 1992, reprinted by permission of The Penguin Group (UK).

p 56 'Eleanor Rigby' words and music by John Lennon and Paul McCartney (Northern Songs / Sony / ATV Music Publishing [UK] Ltd), copyright © John Lennon / Paul McCartney 1966, reprinted by permission of the publisher.

p 58 Extract from *Paperweight* by Stephen Fry (Heinemann, 1992), reprinted by permission of David Higham Associates.

Although every effort has been made to contact copyright holders before publication, this has not always been possible. If notified, the publisher undertakes to rectify any errors or omissions at the earliest opportunity.

Crown copyright material from DfES 0135 / 2002 is reproduced under Class Licence number C01P0000148 with the permission of the Controller of HMSO and the Queen's Printer for Scotland.

Contents

TERM 3

UNIT 1 *Making words work*

Attack!

The wind was shaking autumn leaves off all the trees, and the wind chimes on the sycamore began to peal. Polly let her gaze follow the line of the big tree, up and up, until there, between two boughs she saw a lighted window. And in the window the dark figure of a boy. She couldn't see Gwendal's features but she knew that he was watching her.

Polly didn't hear the garden gate swing open, didn't hear the soft footfalls on the grass. She noticed that Gwendal's position had altered, and almost heard a sound come from him. Now he was struggling to open the window. Polly screwed up her eyes and strained to catch what he was saying. The window flew open and Gwendal pointed at something behind her. 'Polly!' he shouted.

Polly turned. Too late. A grey shape streaked past her. A long misty-looking coat swept across the lawn, sending dead leaves whispering into the air.

Polly screamed and Lancelot leapt out of her arms.

I got home twenty minutes later than usual. I dumped my bag in the hall and called up the stairs. 'Polly? Dad? Are you in?'

No response.

(From *Milo's Wolves* by Jenny Nimmo)

Read the passage through and answer the following questions.

1 What is Polly's relationship with Gwendal?

2 Who or what could Lancelot be?

3 What might be happening?

4 Who tells the first part of the story and who tells the last part?

5 Which words or phrases make the attacker seem evil?

6 In the passage, find five nouns, five adjectives, five powerful verbs, and five prepositions.

7 Change the first sentence into two shorter, more dramatic sentences. You may want to leave out some words and change others, e.g. *The man was running* could become *The man ran*.

8 Rewrite the third paragraph, using some adverbs. Think about where in the sentence they should be.

9 Choose a more powerful verb or adjective for the following extracts:
the line of the big tree   *he was watching her*
I got home   *and called up the stairs*

10 Drop a clause into the sentence: *Polly turned.*
For example, *Tim, gripped by panic, ran.*

11 Use the same basic storyline structure to write a similar passage, e.g.
   • Someone is leaving a place and looks back at someone left behind.
   • The person left behind shouts a warning.
   • An attacker appears.
   • Shift in viewpoint and time – 'I reached home an hour later…'

Remember to choose strong adjectives and adverbs, precise nouns, powerful verbs. Try dropping a clause into at least one sentence. Vary sentence length for dramatic effect.

Making sentences work

RATTLESNAKE POLISH

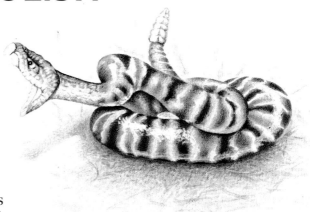

The Warden held up a small jar of dark-red nail polish. "You see this, Caveman?"

He nodded.

"This is my special nail polish. Do you see the dark rich color? You can't buy that in a store. I have to make it myself."

Stanley had no idea why she was showing it to him. He wondered why the Warden would ever have the need to wear nail polish or makeup.

"Do you want to know my secret ingredient?"

He raised and lowered one shoulder.

The Warden opened the bottle. "Rattlesnake venom." With a small paintbrush she began applying it to the nails on her left hand. "It's perfectly harmless...when it's dry." She finished her left hand. She waved it in the air for a few seconds, then began painting the nails on her right hand. "It's only toxic when it's wet."

She finished painting her nails, then stood up. She reached over and touched Stanley's face with her fingers. She ran her sharp wet nails very gently down his cheek. He felt his skin tingle.

The nail on her pinkie just barely touched the wound behind his ear. A sharp sting of pain caused him to jump back. The Warden turned to face Mr. Sir, who was sitting on the fireplace hearth.

"So you think he stole your sunflower seeds?"

"No, he says he stole them, but I think it was —"

She stepped toward him and struck him across the face.

Mr. Sir stared at her. He had three long red marks slanting across the left side of his face. Stanley didn't know if the redness was caused by her nail polish or his blood...

(From *Holes* by Louis Sachar)

Read the passage through and answer the following questions.

1 Find clues that suggest where Stanley might be.

2 Why might he be called 'Caveman'?

3 What has just happened before this incident?

4 Why do you think that the Warden has *the need to wear nail polish?*

5 What might happen next?

6 Why might the Warden have struck Mr. Sir?

7 List examples of the following:
  • one powerful description
  • five powerful verbs
  • one short sentence for impact and clarity
  • one question to focus the reader
  • one compound sentence for flow (using 'and').

8 Which is the most powerful and frightening sentence, and why?

9 Write in the same style a passage featuring the Warden and Stanley.
  Use the following simple sequence of events:
  • The Warden shows Stanley a box.
  • She takes out a jar – inside is a tiny snake.
  • She takes the snake out.
  • Stanley looks at it.
  • She makes him stroke it.
  • She puts the snake away.
  • She warns him to take care – because the snake is deadly!

  Remember to use a variety of sentences. For example:
  • short for impact; compound for flow; complex for extra detail and information
  • questions and exclamations
  • some dialogue balanced by description of what the characters are doing.

Using verbs

Cliff-edge

Then he saw her, just a few feet from him, scrambling through the bracken towards the lighthouse.

'Wait!' he shouted, but she took no notice and ran on, out of her mind with terror. He stumbled after her, still clutching Teddy. She was running as though blind, thrusting the bracken desperately to the side. He followed, calling to her to stop, but she ran on, still screaming. They broke clear of the bracken, the girl just ahead of him, and she raced round the lighthouse fence towards the cliff-edge.

'Stop!' he shouted but still she ran on, arms flailing, head back. The sea yawned before them. 'Stop!' he shouted. 'Stop!'

Then suddenly she wasn't there.

'No!' He shrieked into the wind and kept on running. She couldn't be gone. She couldn't. He heard her voice calling him from below and pelted towards the edge. The land fell away and the sea opened beneath him.

(From *Storm Catchers* by Tim Bowler)

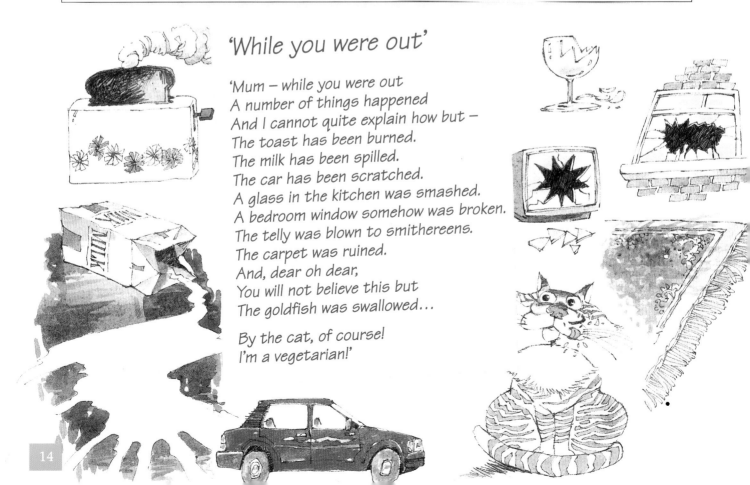

'While you were out'

'Mum – while you were out
A number of things happened
And I cannot quite explain how but –
The toast has been burned.
The milk has been spilled.
The car has been scratched.
A glass in the kitchen was smashed.
A bedroom window somehow was broken.
The telly was blown to smithereens.
The carpet was ruined.
And, dear oh dear,
You will not believe this but
The goldfish was swallowed...

By the cat, of course!
I'm a vegetarian!'

Read the passage and poem through and answer the following questions.

1 How does the girl feel? How do you know?

2 How does the boy feel? How do you know?

3 What effect is the author trying to create?

4 In the poem, who should feel guilty?

5 Which do you prefer out of the passage and poem, and why?

6 From the passage, list the powerful verbs.

7 What is the effect of the verbs?

8 *The toast has been burned* is written in the passive, hiding who actually did it! It could be rewritten as 'I burned the toast'. Rewrite the following in the active:
The car has been scratched.
The carpet was ruined.
The goldfish was swallowed.

9 Use the same basic structure storyline to write a similar passage, for example:
- Main character sees other person.
- Chases them.
- Shouts to her/him.
- He/she disappears.
- Rushes to the place…

Remember to choose powerful verbs and avoid the passive voice.

Using connectives

TOM IN SCHOOL

He sat down upon the end of the pine bench and the girl hitched herself away from him with a toss of her head. Nudges and winks and whispers traversed the room, but Tom sat still, with his arms upon the long, low desk before him, and seemed to study his book.

By and by attention ceased from him, and the accustomed school murmur rose upon the dull air once more. Presently the boy began to steal furtive glances at the girl. She observed it, 'made a mouth' at him and gave him the back of her head for the space of a minute. When she cautiously faced around again, a peach lay before her. She thrust it away. Tom gently put it back. She thrust it away, but with less animosity. Tom patiently returned it to its place. Then she let it remain. Tom scrawled on his slate, *'Please take it – I got more.'* The girl glanced at the words, but made no sign. Now the boy began to draw something on the slate, hiding his work with his left hand. For a time the girl refused to notice, but her human curiosity presently began to manifest itself by hardly perceptible signs. The boy worked on, apparently unconscious. The girl made a sort of noncommittal attempt to see it, but the boy did not betray that he was aware of it. At last she gave in and hesitatingly whispered:

'Let me see it.'

Tom partly uncovered a dismal caricature of a house with two gable ends on it and a corkscrew of smoke issuing from the chimney. Then the girl's interest began to fasten itself upon the work and she forgot everything else. When it was finished, she gazed for a moment, then whispered:

'It's nice – make a man.'

The artist erected a man in the front yard, that resembled a derrick. He could have stepped over the house; but the girl was not hypercritical; she was satisfied with the monster, and whispered:

'It's a beautiful man – now make me coming along.'

Tom drew an hourglass figure with a full moon and straw limbs to it and armed the spreading fingers with a portentous fan. The girl said:

'It's ever so nice – I wish I could draw.'

(From *Tom Sawyer* by Mark Twain)

Read the story through and discuss the following questions.

1 Why do you think Tom sat next to the girl? Explain your reasons.

2 Do you think Tom likes the girl? Give two reasons for your answer.

3 How does Tom engage the girl's interest?

4 Why do you think the writer calls Tom *the boy*?

5 What advice would you give to Tom about what to say or do next? Explain your answer.

6 The writer has used many different connective phrases in this piece. Write a list of the connecting words and phrases.

7 The writer uses the word *whispered* three times. Explain what effect this has on the writing.

8 There are many incidents which happen in school but few people write about them. Select one example from your own experience, or from a story told to you by friends or family, and write about it. Choose whether to write in the first or the third person; explain your choice to your teacher.

Remember to link your ideas using words and phrases, as well as other devices such as repeating words and pronouns. Try to use some of the new phrases from this piece.

Complex sentences (1)

FLYING KICK SPARKS RACING RIOT:

GAIUS IN DEEP TROUBLE AGAIN

Gaius takes a corner three laps into his 39th win.

Rioting chariot racing fans tried to beat three shades of stuffing out of each other at Rome's 250,000 capacity Circus Maximus yesterday. Stadium authorities were forced to call in security staff to restore order.

The trouble started around 3:00pm when fans of the Blue team started to hurl abuse at the Red Team's controversial star driver – hothead Gaius Aquitanius – who had just won his 39th race, and was leaving the stadium in triumph.

As he passed by, Blue fan Scabius Scrumulus shouted out 'Gaius is a girly wimp who gives his horses lumps of sugar and puts pink ribbons on their tails.'

This was clearly too much for Gaius, a slave from Gaul, who leaped into the grandstand and replied with a savage flying head-kick. The incident ignited sections of the crowd, and a close quarters, hand-to-hand brawl erupted in various parts of the stadium. Racing was held up for half an hour while security staff attacked rioters with heavy wooden sticks, and cutting personal remarks.

Interviewed after the incident, Gaius's manager admitted he was angry with his rider. 'I didn't spend 30,000 sesterces buying him from the Greens in order to have him risk an injury attacking some cretin in the crowd. This sport is quite dangerous enough already. If he does it again he'll be whipped. Chariot racing is the nation's number one spectator sport, and this sort of conduct sets a very bad example. If fans want to see competitors behaving like bar-room brawlers they can go to a gladiator arena.'

But Gaius was in no mood to apologise. 'Pah,' he shrugged, 'what can they do? No-one can balance on a flimsy wicker chariot quite like me, or take a corner so tightly without falling off, or control four wild horses with such finesse. My fans are the most loyal in the world, and if my manager has me whipped he'll have all the windows in his town house broken in the middle of the night…'

(Adapted from
The Roman Record by Paul Dowswell)

Read the story through and discuss the following questions.

1 Do you think you would have enjoyed chariot racing?
Explain your answer.

2 Why do you think the supporters started insulting each other?

3 Was Gaius right to attack Scabius?

4 Explain why chariot racing was a dangerous sport.

5 What action do you think Gaius's manager should take?

6 Reread the text, and find two sentences with more than one clause. Write these down.

7 Use these sentences as models for your own sentences about a football match, or another sporting event.

IR

8 Journalists write reports about events like this every day. Write a report for a newspaper on an incident from a recent news programme. Try using a journalistic style; include some complex sentences.

Remember to include details about the participants, and quotations from them. Check the spelling of connecting words you have used.

Complex sentences (2)

ANGLESEY

Covering 276 square miles, **Anglesey** is the largest island in Wales and England. It has been connected with the mainland since 1826, when Thomas Telford built the Menai Bridge, the first heavy-duty suspension bridge to be constructed.

Anglesey is the flattest part of Wales, though there are some rugged cliffs around the coast. It has an interesting coastline with some good sandy beaches. Most visitors, however, see little more than the countryside that surrounds the A5 on the route through to Holyhead and the ferries to Ireland.

- **Anglesey** was a holy place to the ancient Celts and there are still many remains of ancient settlements. Inhabitants since then have relied on farming, smuggling, copper and coal mining, and quarrying, as well as the sea, for their income. The land is very fertile and the island is referred to as Mon Mam Cymru – Mother of Wales – because it provides wheat, cattle and other farm produce for North Wales.

- **Llanfairpwllgwyngyllgogerychwyrndro-bwllllantysiliogogogoch**
  This little village is in the record books as having the longest name of any place in Britain, a sum total of 58 letters. The name means 'St Mary's Church in the hollow of the White Hazel near a rapid whirlpool and the Church of St Tysilio near the Red Cave', and was dreamt up in the 19th century to get the tourists in. At the Tourist Information Centre in the knitwear shop near the station, they'll teach you how to pronounce it.

- **Beaumaris**
  Beaumaris used to be the principal town and chief port of **Anglesey**. It's now known for the castle, and as a sailing and watersports centre. Beaumaris Castle is the last and largest of the castles built by Edward I. Construction started in 1295 on a site overlooking the Menai Strait. The flatness of the site meant the castle could be designed and built with geometrical symmetry – it's truly impressive and it's clear why it's a World Heritage site.
  The castle is surrounded by a water-filled moat, then the outer walls, then evenly spaced towers, then more walls and towers, so it seems impregnable – though Owain Glyndwr did manage to conquer it. The castle last saw action in 1646 during the Civil War.

Read the text through and discuss the following questions.

1 What are the main industries on Anglesey in the 21st century?

2 Why is Anglesey known as the 'Mother of Wales'? Do you think this is a good title?

3 Do you think it was a good idea to give a village such a long name? Explain your answer.

4 Why do you think Beaumaris Castle is a World Heritage site?

5 What would you do if you could spend two days in Anglesey?

6 Rewrite the sentences below which are from the text, changing the order of the clauses. Explain the difference between the two versions.

	Original sentence	Rewritten sentence	Difference between the sentences
a	Anglesey is the flattest part of Wales, though there are some rugged cliffs around the coast.		
b	The land is very fertile and the island is referred to as Mon Mam Cymru – Mother of Wales – because it provides wheat, cattle and other farm produce for North Wales.		
c	At the Tourist Information Centre in the knitwear shop near the station, they'll teach you how to pronounce it.		

7 Write a tourist guide for the area in which you live. Remember to give a general description of the area, and then include details to attract visitors. All the information you give must be accurate. Remember to think carefully about how you order and link clauses in sentences.

Punctuation

Parasitic plants

PARASITIC PLANTS are cheats. Rather than making their own food using the energy from sunlight, they have developed a means of stealing the food made by other plants, known as host plants. Because they do not need sunlight, many parasitic plants spend most of their lives hidden from sight. They attach themselves to the stems or roots of their host plants by means of suckers, known as 'haustoria'. The haustoria penetrate the host's food channels and absorb the sugars and minerals which the parasitic plant needs to live. The world of parasitic plants is a complicated one. Some plants, such as mistletoe, are only partly parasitic, and are known as 'hemiparasites'. These plants have green leaves and so they can use the sun's energy to make some food themselves.

The world's heaviest flower is a species of rafflesia, a parasite which lives on the roots of vines in the jungles of Southeast Asia. Each flower weighs nearly 7kg (15lb) and reaches up to 1m (3ft) in diameter. The flower fills the air with a putrid smell which attracts pollinating flies. The plant is the largest of 50 species, all of them completely parasitic.

There are also parasites in the animal kingdom. Those which affect humans are fleas, headlice, and mosquitoes. These are insects which bite other animals – including humans – and use their blood as food.

Originally a biological term, the word 'parasite' now has a wider meaning: people use it to refer to anyone who does not seem to work, but relies on someone else for their living. Needless to say, it is not a nice term to use about a person!

◀ The heaviest flower in the world – known as the 'stinking giant'

(Adapted from *Plant* by David Burnie)

Read the passage through and discuss the following questions.

1 Why has the writer described parasitic plants as *cheats*? Can you think of any other words to describe them?

2 What effect do you think parasitic plants have on their host plants?

3 Explain in your own words how hemiparasites get their energy.

4 Why do people not like parasites?

5 Why would a person be unhappy about being called a *parasite*?

6 Make a large copy of this table. The writer has used different ways to give additional information, called 'parenthesis'. Look for one example of each. Then find an example of each from another text.

Parenthetic device	Example from 'Parasitic Plants'	Example from another text
commas		
brackets		
dashes		

7 Explain why the writer has used inverted commas (or 'speech marks') in this text, when there is no dialogue.

8 Collect information about a topic on which you have been working, and use this to write a report about it. Remember to keep to the structure of the report, and include as much information as you can.

Think carefully about punctuation. Try to use some punctuation marks you have never used before, including parenthesis, to add detail.

Test preparation (1)

CIRQUE DU FREAK

WE FOUND OURSELVES standing in a long, dark, cold corridor. I had my jacket on, but shivered all the same. It was freezing.

"Why is it so cold?" I asked Steve. It was warm outside.

"Old houses are like that," he told me.

We started to walk. There was a light down by the other end, so the further in we got, the brighter it became. I was glad of that. I don't think I could have made it otherwise: it would have been so scary!

The walls were scratched and scribbled-on, and bits of the ceiling were flaky. It was a creepy place. It would have been bad enough in the middle of the day, but this was ten o'clock, only two hours from midnight!

"There's a door here," Steve said and stopped. He pushed it ajar and it creaked loudly. I almost turned and ran. It sounded like the lid of a coffin being tugged open!

Steve showed no fear and stuck his head in. He said nothing for a few seconds, while his eyes got used to the dark, then pulled back. "It's the stairs up to the balcony," he said.

"Where the kid fell from?" I asked.

"Yes."

"Do you think we should go up?" I asked.

He shook his head. "I don't think so. It's dark up there, no sign of any sort of light. We'll try it if we can't find another way in, but I think —"

"Can I help you boys?" somebody said behind us and we nearly jumped out of our skins!

We turned around quickly and the tallest man in the world was standing there, glaring down on us as if we were a couple of rats. He was so tall, his head almost touched the ceiling. He had huge bony hands and eyes that were so dark, they looked like two black coals stuck in the middle of his face.

"Isn't it late for two little boys like yourselves to be out and about?" he asked. His voice was as deep and croaky as a frog's, but his lips hardly seemed to move. He would have made a great ventriloquist.

"We…" Steve began, but had to stop and lick his lips before he could continue. "We're here to see the Cirque Du Freak," he said.

(From *Cirque Du Freak* by Darren Shan)

Read the passage through and answer the following questions.

1 Describe how the two boys differ in their reaction to the place, giving evidence.

2 List three ways the author makes the place seem frightening.

3 How does Steve try to reassure his friend near the start of the passage?

4 Why did Steve have to *lick his lips*?

5 Find the following:
  • two similes and two well chosen adjectives
  • a question to draw the reader in and an exclamation
  • commas in a descriptive list
  • a short sentence for clarity.

6 Explain whether the words *scary* and *creepy* help to create a frightening effect.

7 Use the same basic storyline to write a similar passage. For example:
  • Two characters are standing in a place they should not have entered.
  • They walk in.
  • They find a door and open it.
  • They decide not to go in.
  • Someone finds them.
  • They give a reason for being there.

Remember:
  • be accurate with your punctuation; use speech marks and commas correctly
  • use effective vocabulary
  • vary your sentences – short, long; simple, compound, complex; question, exclamation.

Test preparation (2)

THE CRUMBLES

You wouldn't notice it. Not unless you were lucky. Skater showed it to me, and that was only because I'd saved his dog when it had tried to dash out onto the A42.

''ere Zip,' he said. 'Wanna come down the Crumbles?' He had already begun to walk on, too quickly for me to keep up. So I jogged beside him. I'd heard of the Crumbles but didn't know anything about them.

'Where's that then?' I asked. Skater didn't reply. So I just tagged along, half walking, half trotting.

We stopped at the top of the avenue. He looked around, and seeing no one in sight, suddenly swung round and pushed on the fencing. A gap appeared and quick as a weasel he squeezed through and was gone.

'Hurry up,' his voice hissed from the other side.

A moment later I was standing on the edge of the Crumbles.

It was an old car dump. A junk-yard that nature had reclaimed. Wrecked cars piled on top of each other like a metallic, giant sandwich. Weeds sprouted through windows. Trees grew up through smashed car bonnets.

Skater beckoned to me from the side of a lorry. He swung up into the cabin and was gone.

I reached up and clambered into the darkness. It smelt musty. The seats had been torn out. I could see Skater's dark shadow in the back of the lorry. He was sitting on an upturned box. 'This is the Crumbles,' he announced. 'It's a secret, like.' I nodded.

A match flared, shadows sprung up around us like spirits. Skater lit a candle and placed it on the floor. We sat on old orange boxes, pretending to warm ourselves by its tiny flame. I thought about my Mam and how she was ill. I looked up at Skater. His eyes seemed too dark. Jet black, like a snake's eyes, I thought.

''Ow's yer Mam, then?' he asked. 'Me Nan says she's not too good. She says to tell yer, it'll be ok. She knows, me Nan does. She's got the sight.' Suddenly his face broke into a smile but then darkened almost instantly. A quick, sudden flash of kindness that he tucked away as soon as it had slipped out.

Read the passage through and answer the following questions.

1 Make two comments about why Skater takes Zip to the Crumbles.

2 What is Zip worried about?

3 How does Skater try to comfort Zip?

4 What does the end suggest about Skater?

5 Find the following in the passage:
  - a simile
  - a short sentence for impact
  - interesting speech that reflects character
  - a good description of the place
  - powerful verbs
  - interesting detail to show character
  - interesting action
  - the most powerful part of the passage.

6 Use the same basic structure and storyline to write a similar passage.
  For example:

  a) A character promises to take someone else to their secret place.
  b) They walk there.
  c) They sneak in.
  d) Character looks around.
  e) They go in somewhere.
  f) They sit.
  g) They talk.

  Remember:
  - be accurate with your punctuation – use speech marks and commas correctly
  - use effective vocabulary – description, details, similes
  - use speech to make the characters distinct
  - make the action interesting
  - vary your sentences – short, long; simple, compound, complex; question, exclamation.

Who dunnit?

MRS SAUVAGE IS UNFLAPPABLE

Mrs Sauvage turned the doorknob and entered La Maison d'Horreur. The door creaked in a suitably frightening fashion. But she didn't care. Nothing scares Mrs Sauvage. She is totally unflappable.

First, she went into the sitting room. It was here that Mr Carruthers had been murdered. Her best hat was blown away.

Then she went into the kitchen. It was here that the cook had died. Her silk scarf was snatched.

After that she went up the stairs. It was here that Mrs Carruthers had died. Her coat was ripped.

Next she walked down to the bathroom. It was here that young Darren was murdered. Her shoes were soaked in water.

Then she made her way to the bedroom. It was here that young Miss Sauvage was killed. Her hands were coated with green slime.

Finally she went up the rickety ladder and into the attic. It was here that the ghost of the house lived. Mrs Sauvage opened the attic window for a breath of fresh air. She admired the view. Yes – she thought, I am totally unflappable. It was then that Mrs Sauvage was pushed.

She tried to flap and fly – but unfortunately she was totally unflappable.

Read the passage through and answer the following questions.

1 What is Mrs Sauvage's big boast?

2 Who do you think carried out the crimes?

3 Who do you think attacked Mrs Sauvage?

4 Explain the play on words in the last line.

5 Explain why you think that the writer uses the passive voice.

6 Turn the following from passive to active.
Her best hat was blown away.
Her hands were coated with green slime.
Her silk scarf was snatched.

7 If you changed the passive sentences into active, how would that change the effect of the story?

8 Use the same repetitive structure, and passive voice, to write in a similar way about a disastrous school trip. Here is the beginning:

Class 6 arrived at 'The Fun Park'. They rushed straight in, whooping and yelling. Poor Mr Hadenough, their weary teacher, followed on behind. The only other visitor was Mr Revenge, an off-duty school inspector.

First they went on the bouncy castle. Darren's shoes were stolen. Mr Hadenough sat on a park bench and dozed.

Formal language (1)

Which job?

Angela's Pet Shop: *Assistant*
—————— £5.50 hourly rate ——————

Angela's Pet Shop recently opened in Camford town centre, specialising in exotic pets. Other pet supplies are also available.

Angela is looking for an energetic person to help in the shop on Saturdays. Duties will include:

- cleaning cages
- feeding and exercising pets
- serving customers
- answering the telephone.

Some training will be offered to successful applicants; however, experience of owning exotic pets will be an advantage.

Please apply by letter, outlining your experience, and giving names of referees to:
Angela, The Pet Shop, Main Street, Camford.

SATURDAY ASSISTANT WANTED

£33 per day!!

Are you fit, energetic and willing to learn?
If so, read on...

Assistant needed for town centre car wash. Applicants must be hard-working and have good literacy and numeracy skills.

The assistant will be required to:

wash and wax cars

valet car interiors

References required. No time-wasters.
Application forms from:
Wash'n'Wax, Camford Rd, Camford. Tel: 01456 382 382

Read the advertisements through and discuss the following questions.

1 Which of these jobs would suit someone who collects lizards? Explain.

2 Both these jobs need a lot of energy. Explain why.

3 Explain why references are required for both posts.

4 Explain why literacy and numeracy skills are important. Why has Angela not specifically asked for literacy skills?

5 Which of these jobs you would prefer? Explain why.

6 Here are some phrases taken from the adverts. Make a large copy of this table and, for each phrase, compose one sentence that is less formal and one that is more formal.

Informal	Original	Very formal
	Assistant needed for town centre car wash.	
	Angela is looking for an energetic person to help in the shop on Saturdays.	
	Applicants must be hard-working and have good literacy and numeracy skills.	
	Are you fit, energetic and willing to learn?	

7 Write an advertisement for a job. Remember to structure the advertisement, and use formal language. Make sure that you include all necessary information.

NOTICE OF INTENTION:
16th February 2003

NOTICE IS HEREBY GIVEN that the Engleford Town Council intend not less than seven days from the date hereof to make an order, the effect of which will be to prohibit traffic in either direction along part of the A8040 Tarbin Crossroads to Dengy Rd from its junction with the A88(T) Headly Rd in a southerly direction to its junction with the Class III road at Dengy.

The Order is necessary because of works necessary in the construction of the new A808 Expressway.

The alternative route:

Traffic approaching from the A88 Clarry junction will be diverted along the A88 road in a westerly direction to its junction with the Chapel Class III Lamblet to Lenfelg road. Traffic will then proceed along the Class III road in a southerly direction to its junction with the A8040 road. Traffic travelling the A8040 shall use the reverse of the above route.

The Order comes into effect at 7:00pm on 23/02/03 and will continue in force for a period not exceeding three months or until the work which it is proposed to carry out on the road is completed, whichever is the earlier. At this stage it is anticipated that the work will be completed in less than 6 hours.

For further information regarding the above, please telephone the legal section at Engleford Town Council

ETC

Read the text through and discuss the following questions.

1 Why is the town council banning traffic from this road?

2 How long do you think the ban will last? Explain your answer.

3 Do you think drivers will mind about the problem? Explain your answer.

4 Why do you think this notice was printed in local newspapers?

5 How else might drivers find out about this arrangement?

6 Look at the following sentences from the text. Make a large copy of the table and rewrite the sentences to make them easier to understand. Be careful with your punctuation.

The Order is necessary because of works necessary in the construction of the new A808 Expressway.	
Traffic travelling the A8040 shall use the reverse of the above route.	
The Order comes into effect at 7:00pm on 23/02/03 and will continue in force for a period not exceeding three months or until the work which it is proposed to carry out on the road is completed, whichever is the earlier.	
At this stage it is anticipated that the work will be completed in less than 6 hours.	

7 Write a public notice for display in your school. Write two versions: a formal and a more user-friendly one.

Remember to use formal, impersonal language in the first notice. Be careful with your punctuation.

Complex sentences (4)

Mr. Jabez Wilson

The portly client puffed out his chest with an appearance of some little pride and pulled a dirty and wrinkled newspaper from the inside pocket of his greatcoat. As he glanced down the advertisement column, with his head thrust forward and the paper flattened out upon his knee, I took a good look at the man and endeavoured, after the fashion of my companion, to read the indications which might be presented by his dress or appearance.

I did not gain very much, however, by my inspection. Our visitor bore every mark of being an average commonplace British tradesman, obese, pompous, and slow. He wore rather

baggy grey shepherd's check trousers, a not over-clean black frock-coat, unbuttoned in the front, and a drab waistcoat with a heavy brassy Albert chain, and a square pierced bit of metal dangling down as an ornament. A frayed top-hat and a faded brown overcoat with a wrinkled velvet collar lay upon a chair beside him. Altogether, look as I would, there was nothing remarkable about the man save his blazing red head, and the expression of extreme chagrin and discontent upon his features.

Sherlock Holmes's quick eye took in my occupation, and he shook his head with a smile as he noticed my questioning glances.

'Beyond the obvious facts that he has at some time done manual labour, that he takes snuff, that he is a Freemason, that he has been in China, and that he has done a considerable amount of writing lately, I can deduce nothing else.'

Mr. Jabez Wilson started up in his chair, with his forefinger upon the paper, but his eyes upon my companion.

'How, in the name of good-fortune, did you know all that, Mr. Holmes?' he asked. 'How did you know, for example, that I did manual labour. It's as true as gospel, for I began as a ship's carpenter.'

(From *The Red-Headed League* by Arthur Conan Doyle)

Read the story through and discuss the following questions.

1 What did Dr Watson think about Mr Wilson?

2 Do you think Mr Wilson was a rich person? Explain your answer.

3 How do you think Mr Wilson felt when Sherlock Holmes found out so much about him?

4 How do you think Dr Watson felt when Mr Wilson agreed with Sherlock Holmes?

5 Why do you think Mr Wilson has come to see Sherlock Holmes? What clues are there?

6 Find and copy out two sentences which are lists.

7 Find and copy out two sentences which have connectives at the beginning.

8 Make a list of the connectives used in this text.

9 Can you write like Arthur Conan Doyle? Write a part of a story where two old friends meet someone new and form completely different ideas about her/him. Write the story from the point of view of one of the friends.

Contracting sentences

Hiding from the Martians

ON THE TWELFTH DAY my throat was so painful that, taking the chance of alarming the Martians, I attacked the creaking rain-water pump that stood by the sink, and got a couple of glassfuls of blackened and tainted rain water. I was greatly refreshed by this, and emboldened by the fact that no enquiring tentacle followed the noise of my pumping.

During these days, in a rambling, inconclusive way, I thought much of the curate and of the manner of his death.

On the thirteenth day I drank some more water, and dozed and thought disjointedly of eating and of vague impossible plans of escape. Whenever I dozed I dreamt of horrible phantasms, of the death of the curate, or of sumptuous dinners; but, asleep or awake, I felt a keen pain that urged me to drink again and again. The light that came into the scullery was no longer grey, but red. To my disordered imagination it seemed the colour of blood.

On the fourteenth day I went into the kitchen, and I was surprised to find that the fronds of the red weed had grown right across the hole in the wall, turning the half-light of the place into a crimson-coloured obscurity.

It was early on the fifteenth day that I heard a curious, familiar sequence of sounds in the kitchen, and, listening, identified it as the snuffing and scratching of a dog. Going into the kitchen, I saw a dog's nose peering in through a break among the ruddy fronds. This greatly surprised me. At the scent of me he barked shortly.

I thought if I could induce him to come into the place quietly I should be able, perhaps, to kill and eat him; and in any case, it would be advisable to kill him, lest his actions attracted the attention of the Martians.

(From *The War of the Worlds* by H.G. Wells)

Read the story through and discuss the following questions.

1 Why do you think the narrator is hiding?

2 What would be the worst thing about hiding like this?

3 How do you think the narrator felt when he heard the dog?

4 Give two reasons why the narrator thought he should kill the dog.

5 What do you think the narrator did next?

6 There is a lot of detail in this passage. Make a large copy of the table and rewrite these sentences in note form. The first one has been done for you.

Sentence	Notes
On the thirteenth day I drank some more water, and dozed and thought disjointedly of eating and of vague impossible plans of escape.	*Day 13: drank water, thought about eating and escaping*
It was early on the fifteenth day that I heard a curious, familiar sequence of sounds in the kitchen, and, listening, identified it as the snuffing and scratching of a dog.	
I thought if I could induce him to come into the place quietly I should be able, perhaps, to kill and eat him; and in any case, it would be advisable to kill him, lest his actions attracted the attention of the Martians.	

7 Now rewrite the whole passage in note form. Remember that you can probably leave out some sentences.

8 H.G. Wells was writing about hiding from Martians who had taken over the world. Write a similar passage about hiding from a strange creature. Try to use some of the sentence structures that Wells uses, to make it sound like Wells' own writing.

Conditionals

Dental safety

I have heard that fluoride can help stop dental decay, but I recently read that it is poisonous. Which of these is true? How can children use fluoride safely?

This question is answered by Dr Marcia M. Rich who practises general dentistry in Newholt. She is also a lecturer at the University and a writer for the monthly magazine Your Dentist Cares.

My answer to the first question is to stress that fluoride works well and is safe when users follow instructions. Young children have a tendency to swallow toothpaste, which is why they should only have a tiny amount of fluoride toothpaste on their toothbrush. If this simple precaution is taken, parents can be confident that children will be protected against tooth decay, and come to no harm.

Almost all medicines can have an adverse effect – or even be deadly – if they are not taken as directed. So you are right – fluoride can be poisonous if it is swallowed in very large quantities. It is for this reason that fluoride supplements can only be obtained on prescription from a doctor or dentist. Please be assured that fluoride overdoses are rare – in fact, I have never heard of any fatal incidents related to fluoride poisoning.

Scientific studies have shown that fluoride can help to prevent cavities as long as it is used correctly. If fluoride is abused, there is a risk of illness or even death in extreme cases. If a lethal amount of fluoride is ingested, immediate first-aid could save a life. A person who has swallowed a large amount of fluoride will probably start vomiting. If not, vomiting should be induced. The patient should be given milk or antacid and taken to the nearest hospital for emergency treatment.

The ingestion of too much fluoride while teeth are growing can lead to a condition called dental fluorosis. The most likely cause is the swallowing of fluoride toothpastes by young children. It can also be caused by the inappropriate use of fluoride drops or other fluoride supplements, for example when fluoride is already present in drinking water.

Read the text through and discuss the following questions.

1 Why is fluoride useful for children?

2 Has anyone ever died from an overdose of fluoride?

3 What should you do if someone takes too much fluoride?

4 Give two ways in which people can take fluoride.

5 Why do you think the writer's qualifications and experience are included before her answer?

6 Find at least three sentences with conditional clauses. If you have any problem, remember that they will probably include the word *if*. Copy these sentences out.

7 Some of the sentences can be rewritten using *unless* or *as long as*. Try rewriting your sentences. Do they make sense? Has the meaning changed? Which versions do you think work best?

8 You are going away with your aunt and uncle for a weekend. The journey will be about 60 miles (100 kilometres). Consider whether you should travel by car or by train. Begin by writing a list of reasons. Then write an answer from your point of view.

Revision (1) – narrative writing

Prequel

Samantha was loved by everyone who knew her; she, in turn, loved soccer. She watched soccer, read about soccer, talked about soccer, played soccer. It was her whole life. So when the school team selection was posted – and she was not on it – her world fell apart.

Although supported by her friends and family, Samantha spent the whole night in tears, even missing Match of the Day. Her homework was not done, and someone else had to walk the dog. Samantha was inconsolable.

The next morning, Samantha's friends waited for her as usual, but she was nowhere to be seen. As they walked along, they wondered whether she would be coming in to school at all. What would she do now, what would she be thinking? None of them could even imagine.

Samantha arrived in school just before registration. She walked calmly into school, and went to sit down next to Chastity. Her friends exchanged nervous glances: she was <u>too</u> calm. Something was going to happen – but what?

At breaktime, Samantha was left alone. She sat in a corner, reading quietly. No-one knew quite what to do.

Read the story through and discuss the following questions.

1 This story is called 'Prequel'. What does this mean?

2 What emotions do you think Samantha would experience when she was not selected for the team?

3 What do you think Samantha's friends thought might have happened to her when she didn't meet them in the morning?

4 Why did they exchange *nervous glances*? Explain as fully as you can.

5 What do you think might happen next?

6 The writer has used many passive forms in this text. Find at least three sentences with passive verbs, and underline the passives.

7 Some sentences work as either active or passive. Others don't. Take a look at the following pairs of sentences, and decide which ones seem to work.

Samantha loved football.	Football was loved by Samantha.
Samantha's parents loved her.	Samantha was loved by her parents.

Write passive forms of the following sentences:
Sariah did her homework.
Curtis fed the fish.
Jabriel met his friends.
Tick the ones which make sense in the passive form.

8 Carry on with this story. Remember that you can use passive and active forms.

Revision (2) – formal writing

Uniform Approach

School uniforms are a regular subject of debate – Rachel Clews found out what people think

Uniforms have long been a way of establishing a corporate identity in Britain, but how do people really feel about them?

In response to the widely-differing views on uniform, many schools are now giving their students a voice.

For example, the student council at St. John Bosco High School, Croxteth, has been running for several years and headteacher Sr. Helen Murphy is enthusiastic about the results. She said that one achievement of the council had been its input into uniform changes.

Student councils are becoming similarly popular with primary schools. Mrs McDonell, headteacher of St Matthew's Junior School said: "We are hoping that the student council will be a forum for pupils to express their ideas."

One topic that sparks varied responses is the issue of summer and winter uniforms, particularly the option to wear summer dresses. Mrs Zimak, headteacher at Archbishop Blanch, told us: "We took a vote, and there were only three or four who wanted them." On the other hand, Mr Baker, headteacher at Croxteth Community Comprehensive, said that the school decision on summer dresses came after requests from parents. But he added: "As they may be too expensive for some parents, they were to remain as an optional summer outfit."

The introduction of trousers for girls brings similar differences of opinion. Many girls said that trousers were a lot more comfortable and not as restricting as skirts, but many schools are still resisting change and many girls feel that they should be given the choice.

On trousers, though, Mr Baker said: "We have never seen any reason to dissuade them from it, as long as they aren't the height of fashion." However, Mr Yates of St Hilda's High School said: "It's a girls' school and the uniform says it has to be a skirt."

Recent years have seen a rise in the popularity of non-uniform days. However, Sr. Helen Murphy is not convinced about them. She said: "Although they are a good fundraiser, they encourage a more sinister kind of bullying such as looking down your nose at people."

For this reason many schools are now phasing out non-uniform days, although with pupils they are still very popular.

> EDITOR'S NOTE: What do Pressgang *readers think about school uniforms? Do you think they are important or do you think there should be more freedom? Write and let us know.*

(Adapted from *Pressgang,* a magazine written and edited by children in Liverpool)

Read the article through and discuss the following questions.

1 At least two schools quoted here have a school council. Do you think this is a good idea? Explain your answer.

2 Give one reason for and one reason against having a summer uniform.

3 Give two reasons from the article why girls might prefer to wear trousers to school.

4 Why do you think Mr Baker discourages girls from wearing trousers which are *the height of fashion*?

5 Sister Helen Murphy thinks some pupils may be upset by non-uniform days. Do you agree with her? Explain your answer.

6 Identify one sentence in the text which contains a conditional. Rephrase it using *if …, then…* .

7 Compose four conditional sentences of your own about school uniform, using ideas different from those expressed in the article.

8 *EDITOR'S NOTE: What do* Pressgang *readers think about school uniforms? Do you think they are important or do you think there should be more freedom? Write and let us know.*

What do you think? What do your parents think? Who else would be interested in this issue? Write an argument in favour of or against school uniforms. Try to use as many ideas as possible, but keep your language formal – and remember that you want to persuade readers to agree with you.

UNIT 18 *Test preparation (3)*

I, Kensuke

He was diminutive, no taller than me, and as old a man as I had ever seen. He wore nothing but a pair of tattered breeches bunched at the waist, and there was a large knife in his belt. He was thin, too. In places – under his arms, round his neck and his midriff – his copper brown skin lay in folds about him, almost as if he'd shrunk inside it. What little hair he had on his head and his chin was long and wispy and white.

I could see at once that he was very agitated, his chin trembling, his heavily hooded eyes accusing and angry. *'Dameda! Dameda!'* he screeched at me. His whole body was shaking with fury. I backed away as he scuttled up the beach towards me, gesticulating wildly with his stick, and haranguing me as he came. Ancient and skeletal he may have been, but he was moving fast, running almost. *'Dameda! Dameda!'* I had no idea what he was saying. It sounded Chinese or Japanese, maybe.

I was about to turn and run when Stella, who, strangely, had not barked at him at all, suddenly left my side and went bounding off towards him. Her hackles were not up. She was not growling. To my astonishment she greeted him like a long lost friend.

He was no more than a few feet away from me when he stopped. We stood looking at each other in silence for a few moments. He was leaning on his stick, trying to catch his breath. 'Americajin? Americajin? American? *Eikokujin?* British?'

'Yes,' I said, relieved to have understood something at last. 'English, I'm English.'

It seemed a struggle for him to get the words out. 'No good. Fire, no good. You understand? No fire.' He seemed less angry now.

'But my mother, my father, they might see it, see the smoke.' It was plain he didn't understand me. So I pointed out to sea, by way of explanation. 'Out there. They're out there. They'll see the fire. They'll come and fetch me.'

Instantly he became aggressive again. *'Dameda!'* he shrieked, waving his stick at me. 'No fire!' I thought for a moment he was going to attack me, but he did not. Instead he began to rake through the sand at my feet with his stick. He was drawing the outline of something, jabbering incomprehensibly all the time. It looked like some kind of a fruit at first, a nut perhaps, a peanut. Now I understood. It was a map of the island. When it was done he fell on his knees beside it, and piled up mounds of sand, one at each end – the two hills. Then, very deliberately, he etched out a straight line, top to bottom, cutting the smaller end of the island off from the larger one.

(From *Kensuke's Kingdom* by Michael Morpurgo)

Read the story through and discuss the following questions.

1 How do you think the narrator felt about the old man when he first met him? Explain your answer.

2 Why do you think the dog greets the old man?

3 Why do you think the old man did not want the boy to light a fire?

4 The narrator says that the old man was *jabbering incomprehensibly.* There is more than one way to think of this. Give at least two reasons why his speech seemed like this.

5 Why do you think the old man has drawn a map and divided it? How would that make the boy feel?

6 Make a large copy of the table. For each paragraph, explain what its purpose is, and how it is linked to the previous one. Remember that sometimes a change of speaker in dialogue will trigger a new paragraph.

Paragraph	Purpose	Link to previous paragraph
1	*Physical description*	*Start of description*
2		
3		
4		
5		
6		
7		
8		

8 This passage is about the first meeting between two characters who have difficulty understanding each other. Write about a similar encounter, imagined or real, between yourself and another person.

Remember to use paragraphs to divide your story into sections. Help your readers by linking the paragraphs. You could use some ideas from Michael Morpurgo's story.

ORPHEUS IN HADES

He came to a pair of gates a mile high, the spiked points rising higher than the mountain, brushing the very clouds. The gates were made of black iron, with iron skulls set between the twisting bars. A brazier burned on each side, the flames as cold as ice. Behind the gates he could just make out an enormous cavern, a great circle of darkness. This was the entrance to Hades. And it was guarded.

A dog lumbered out of the shadows, growling softly at Orpheus, with not one but three heads. Its three mouths hung open, black venom dripping over needle-sharp teeth. The dog was huge, bigger than a horse. Its black fur hung in knots off its deformed body as if it had rolled in tar. Now it squatted, preparing to pounce. One of the heads began to howl, the horrible sound rising to a pitch and threatening to crack open the mountain itself. The other heads snapped at the air, the necks straining, the eyes bulging with hatred and fear.

Slowly, Orpheus lifted the lyre. The howling stopped. One of the heads sniffed at him suspiciously. He began to play.

The sound was tiny, lost in that eternal wilderness, but still the dog heard it. It fell silent and the muscles in its neck relaxed. One of the heads made a last protest, barking feebly, but at once the other two turned on it, tearing at its ears and cheeks with their teeth. It yelped, then listened quietly. Orpheus continued to play, louder now, the music swelling up like a blossom opening. Never had such a sound been heard at the gateway of Hades. The dog sank to the ground. Something close to pleasure flickered in its yellow eyes. Two of the heads nodded and fell asleep. The third sighed, then joined them. Orpheus played until he reached the end of the song. By then the dog was sound asleep, its tail twitching, its three heads snoring in unison. Gently, he stepped round it. The gates opened and he passed through.

(From 'Orpheus in the Underworld' in *The Kingfisher Book of Myths and Legends* retold by Anthony Horowitz)

Read the story through and discuss the following questions.

1 What sort of story is this (e.g. ghost story, legend, myth, adventure story, fable)? Give evidence to support your answer.

2 Is there anything unusual about the entrance to Hades?

3 How do you think Orpheus felt when he saw the dog? How do you know?

4 Do you think the animal is one dog with three heads, or three dogs with only one body? Explain your answer.

5 Why do you think Orpheus played until he reached the end of the song?

6 There is a great deal of descriptive language in this extract, including some simile and metaphor. Select the three examples of descriptive language that you think are the most effective, and explain why. You may choose a word, a phrase or a sentence.

7 Write three descriptive sentences about things you have experienced, based on the three examples you have selected from this text.

8 Select one of the options below:

a) Rewrite this passage as a recount from a newspaper. Remember to include the sorts of feature you might expect to find in a newspaper report – quotes, details about the individuals, headlines, etc.

b) Select a newspaper story to rewrite as a myth, with a wealth of descriptive language. Remember that you can add details, and that the story does not need to be realistic.

Comparing text types (2)

How on Earth do volcanoes erupt?

1 Deep underground in the mantle, magma rises upwards. It rises because it's mixed with gas so it's lighter than the rocks around it. To see how the magma rises, try this edible experiment:

What you will need:
- two corks (for the magma)
- a jar of honey (for the rocks)

What you do:
a) Push the corks into the honey so they are completely covered.
b) Watch them bob upwards. Just like magma (well, almost).
c) Spread the honey on toast and eat it. (Take the corks out first.)

2 The magma rises into the crust. As it squeezes and pushes its way up, the pressure mounts. The gases inside it bubble and fizz (like a can of pop if you shake it). The pressure goes up…

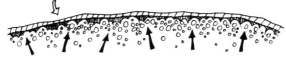

3 And up … and up.

4 … until, one day, the magma and gas rush upwards, burst out through cracks in the crust, and erupt. (As the pop will when you open the can, so be warned.)

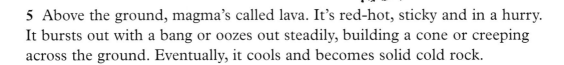

5 Above the ground, magma's called lava. It's red-hot, sticky and in a hurry. It bursts out with a bang or oozes out steadily, building a cone or creeping across the ground. Eventually, it cools and becomes solid cold rock.

(From *Violent Volcanoes* by Anita Ganeri)

Read the text through and discuss the following questions.

1 What sort of text is this?

2 Explain why the writer has put an experiment in the middle.

3 Is this text written for adults or children? Explain your answer.

4 List three things that the writer has done to help readers understand how volcanoes erupt.

5 What part of the text did you find most helpful?

 6 What other type of text is 'embedded' in this explanation?

7 Make a large copy of the table and then fill it in.

Features of explanatory texts	Found in this text?	Example from this text
Introduction		
Sequence of steps		
Simple present tense (usually)		
Logical connectives		
Time connectives		
Formal voice		
Diagram/photograph		

8 In this text there are connectives of **time** and connectives of **logic**. Make a list of each.

9 This explanation has been written in a very informal way. Find out as much as you can about volcanoes and how they erupt. Use this and the information already in the text to write a more formal explanation of the process.

Comparing text types (3)

FREEFALL

The heavier an object is, the faster it falls – right? Not quite! Take three identical A4 sheets of paper. Fold one, screw one into a ball and leave one flat, then drop them from shoulder height. They don't drop at the same rate, do they?

Why is this? There is more than one force acting on falling objects. Gravity is the obvious one – that's the force that makes objects fall. So, there must be another force at work.

To understand this, it is necessary to work out which object took longest to fall. It was the flat piece of paper. This is because of air resistance – the paper has to 'push air out of the way' as it falls, so the larger the surface area of the paper, the longer this will take. The air resistance works in the opposite direction to gravity, providing up-thrust.

This is a very important principle – it explains how parachutes work. Can you think of anything else?

Read the text through and discuss the following questions.

1 What sort of text is this? Give reasons for your answer.

2 Do you think this text has been written for an adult or a child? Explain your answer.

3 How does the force of gravity act upon the paper?

4 Explain in your own words how the force of air resistance acts upon the paper.

5 How does this make parachutes work?

6 Find two examples of sentences written in the second person and two examples of sentences written in the impersonal voice. Copy them down.

7 Rewrite these sentences in the impersonal voice / second person.

8 Explain why you think the writer has used the second person at the beginning and the end of the piece, and the impersonal voice in the middle sections.

9 Write an explanation for other children of your age. Base it on a process with which you are familiar, or which you have recently explored in science – for example, why some objects float.

UNIT

22 *Formal language (2)*

Building child friendly communities

"The communities are not safe as we hang around on the streets, nowhere to go. And that's why we get the blame for damage, fights and abuse – it's not our fault, it's yours, you make the problems."

15 year old from the South East.

- More than 40,000 children a year are killed or injured on our roads, and the UK has one of the worst child pedestrian death rates in Europe.
- Almost two-thirds of 12 to 15 year olds have suffered some form of victimisation during the past six to eight months.
- One in three has been assaulted on some occasion in the same period.

To make sure that children are safe in the community we need:

- more neighbourhood wardens, park rangers and police on the beat
- a target of 1,000 Home Zones in the next five years, with safe, low speed limits and a legal right of way for pedestrians
- a Quiet Roads initiative in rural areas giving priority to cyclists and pedestrians
- safe Travel Routes to allow children to get to schools, parks, shops and stations
- money to pay for youth work
- a law that local authorities must measure the needs of children and families living in rural isolation, and show how they are meeting the needs of these people

(Adapted from *Our children, their future – A manifesto* on www.nspcc.org.uk)

Read the text through and discuss the following questions.

1 Why do you think the writers chose this quotation?

2 Describe the three main problems in your own words.

3 Which of the suggestions to improve road safety do you think is most important? Explain your answer.

4 What problems might children living in *rural isolation* have?

5 Why do you think it would be helpful to increase the numbers of:
 • neighbourhood wardens   • park rangers   • police on the beat?

6 Rewrite these passive sentences in the active mood:
 a) *More than 40,000 children a year are killed or injured on our roads, and the UK has one of the worst child pedestrian death rates in Europe.*
 b) *One in three has been assaulted on some occasion in the same period.*

7 Why have the writers chosen the passive form for these sentences?

8 We can make sentences using the bullet points, for example:
To make sure that children are safe in the community we need a law that local authorities must measure the needs of children and families living in rural isolation, and show how they are meeting the needs of these people.

Select and rewrite two other bullet points.

9 Discuss with your class other problems facing children today. Write another section of a manifesto which
 a) describes the problems
 b) uses a quote to give children's point of view
 c) makes some recommendations for improving the situation.

Remember to use a formal tone. You should write in the present tense. Try to use some passive forms, complex sentences and an impersonal tone. Your writing should persuade other people to agree with you!

Complex sentences (5)

THE LAST GAME

I could find it in me to forgive them for coming so close and blowing it: they were young, and they'd had a fantastic season and as a supporter you cannot really ask for more than that.

I got excited when we scored right at the beginning of the second half, and I got excited again about ten minutes from time, when Thomas had a clear chance and hit it straight at Grobbelaar, but Liverpool seemed to be growing stronger and to be creating chances at the end, and finally, with the clock in the corner of the TV screen showing that the ninety minutes had passed, I got ready to muster a brave smile for a brave team. 'If Arsenal are to lose the Championship, having had such a lead at one time, it's somewhat poetic justice that they have got a result on the last day, even though they're not to win it,' said co-commentator David Pleat as Kevin Richardson received treatment for an injury with the Kop already celebrating. 'They will see that as scant consolation, I should think, David,' replied Brian Moore. Scant consolation indeed, for all of us.

Richardson finally got up, ninety-two minutes gone now, and even managed a penalty-area tackle on John Barnes; then Lukic bowled the ball out to Dixon, Dixon on, inevitably, to Smith, a brilliant Smith flick-on ... and suddenly, in the last minute of the last game of the season, Thomas was through, on his own, with a chance to win the Championship for Arsenal. 'It's up for grabs now!' Brian Moore yelled; and even then I found that I was reining myself in, learning from recent lapses in hardened scepticism, thinking, well, at least we came close at the end there, instead of thinking, please Michael, please.

Michael, please put it in, please God let him score. And then he was turning a somersault, and I was flat out on the floor, and everybody in the living room jumped on top of me. Eighteen years, all forgotten in a second.

(From *Fever Pitch* by Nick Hornby)

Read the story through and discuss the following questions.

1 Why is this an important match? Find evidence from the text.

2 How do you think Nick Hornby felt during the first half of the match?

3 What two emotions did Hornby feel watching Thomas's shot?

4 Do you think Hornby saw Michael Thomas actually score? Explain your answer.

5 In your own words, explain what you think the final sentence means.

6 The first sentence of the second paragraph of this excerpt is particularly long and complex. Try to rewrite it as two or more shorter sentences.
   When you have done this, write down why you think Nick Hornby wrote this as one long sentence, and whether you think it is successful. Give at least one reason for your answer.

7 Describe two features of Nick Hornby's style of writing which you have seen in this excerpt. Give examples of both.

8 Write an account of a football match, or other sporting event, in the style of Nick Hornby. You may need to watch an event on TV, as Nick Hornby did, or collect various newspaper reports, listen to a radio commentary, talk to others who attended or watched the event and so on.

   Remember – try to make it exciting by using as many of Hornby's strategies as you can.

Eleanor Rigby

Ah, look at all the lonely people!
Ah, look at all the lonely people!

Eleanor Rigby,
picks up the rice in the church where a
wedding has been,
lives in a dream.
Waits at the window,
wearing the face that she keeps in a jar
by the door,
who is it for?

All the lonely people,
where do they all come from?
All the lonely people,
where do they all belong?

Father McKenzie,
writing the words of a sermon that no
one will hear,
no one comes near.
Look at him working,
darning his socks in the night when
there's nobody there,
what does he care?

All the lonely people,
where do they all come from?
All the lonely people,
where do they all belong?

Ah, look at all the lonely people!
Ah, look at all the lonely people!

Eleanor Rigby,
died in the church and was buried along
with her name.
Nobody came.
Father McKenzie,
wiping the dirt from his hands as he
walks from the grave,
no one was saved.

All the lonely people,
where do they all come from?
All the lonely people,
where do they all belong?

John Lennon & Paul McCartney

Read the lyrics through and discuss the following questions.

1 What do you think Eleanor Rigby looked like? Write a brief description of her.

2 How could Eleanor Rigby keep her face *in a jar by the door*?

3 Why was Eleanor Rigby's name buried along with her? What does this mean?

4 How do you think Father McKenzie might have felt at Eleanor Rigby's funeral? Explain why you think that.

5 How did you feel when you finished reading the lyrics of this song? Do you think this is how the writers intended you to feel?

6 Look at these sentences:
Look at all this mess.
We all saw it.

Decide whether the writer is using the word *all* literally or not.

7 There are other ways of emphasizing a point. Write down three that you use in everyday speech or in your own writing.

8 Use the structure of this poem to write another – this time dealing with a different emotion, such as happiness, sadness or tiredness.

Remember to use details from which listeners/readers can learn a lot about the individuals involved. You will need to emphasize their plight.

Developing a style

ZOO TIME

IN MY SALAD DAYS, when I was green in judgment and tossed in a light vinaigrette of faith, I liked nothing better than to put my trusting little hand in that of my mother and toddle to the zoo. The possibility of pandas and the likelihood of woolly monkeys exerted the strongest of pulls. But then, in my pudding days, when I was starchier in judgment and steeped in a heavy syrup of doubt, I found myself wondering dreadfully. Was it not possible that future generations would look back with amazement and distaste at our casual willingness to countenance the imprisonment of animals?

This whole question of the refinement of moral values is an interesting one. Perfectly virtuous, kind and considerate people two hundred years ago kept slaves, owned shares in sugar plantations that used nothing but slaves and wore cotton that they knew perfectly well had been picked by slaves. If you were to tell them that they were participating in, encouraging and prolonging one of the most noxious and inhuman practices conceivable they would have thought you mad.

More recently our grandfathers or great-grandfathers would have snorted with astonishment and distaste if told that withholding the vote from one half of the population gave lie to claims that Britain was a democracy. Those who campaigned for feminine suffrage were hysterical, women didn't understand politics, they should never, never be allowed to vote, the majority of men argued. If you were then to tell them that in sixty years' time Britain's longest serving Prime Minister would be a woman they would probably have gone into spasm.

But our grandfathers were not wicked, nor too stupid to grasp the moral arguments that we now take for granted. Morality after all is custom and we are accustomed to the idea that it is wrong for one human to own another, that it is inimical for women to be denied a vote and, for instance, that bear baiting and freak shows are disgusting.

(From *Paperweight* by Stephen Fry)

Read the text through and discuss the following questions.

1 Has Stephen Fry always liked zoos? How do you know?

2 What other issues does Stephen Fry cover in this extract?

3 Why do you think he links these issues with zoos?

4 Why do you think Stephen Fry has written this article?

5 Is Stephen Fry writing for adults or children? How can you tell?

 6 Note three things you notice about Stephen Fry's style of writing. Use these features to explain whether or not you enjoyed the piece.

7 Write down your three favourite phrases from this extract.

 8 Write a persuasive piece about zoos – either in favour of them or against them. You may find it useful to carry out some research, including interviews with people who have opinions about zoos.

Remember to structure the piece well and support your views with evidence.

Glossary

active and passive   Verbs can be active or passive, e.g. *The queen ate the tarts* (active); *The tarts were eaten* (passive).
In an **active** sentence the subject (*the queen*) performs the action (*ate the tarts*). In a **passive** sentence, the subject (*tarts*) is on the receiving end of the action. In the passive you can hide who did the action.

adjective   An adjective is a word that describes somebody or something.
1 Adjectives are usually found in front of a noun.
   For example: *green* emeralds and *glittering* diamonds
2 In some cases, adjectives can come after a verb.
   For example: It was *big*.
3 Sometimes you can use two adjectives together, e.g. *tall and handsome*. This is called an **adjectival phrase**.
4 Adjectives can be used to describe degrees of intensity. To make a **comparative** adjective you usually add *er* (or use *more*).
   For example: *quick/quicker   more beautiful*
5 To make a **superlative** you add *est* (or use *most*).
   For example: *quickest   most beautiful*

adverb   An adverb adds further meaning to a verb. Many are formed by adding *ly* to an adjective, e.g. *slow/slowly*. They often come next to the verb in a sentence. Adverbs can tell the reader:
How: *quickly, stupidly, amazingly.*   Where: *there, here, everywhere.*
When: *yesterday, today, now.*   How often: *occasionally, often.*

agreement   Agreement is the link between the subject of a sentence and the verb.
For example: *I am/I was   You are/you were*
                 The storm was becoming worse   The storms were becoming worse

apostrophe   An apostrophe (') is a punctuation mark that is used in two ways:
1 To show where letters are missing, e.g. *don't, can't, I'm.*
2 To show possession, e.g. *my dog's collar*. This explains that the collar belongs to my dog. In the plural the apostrophe follows the *s*, e.g. *the boys' cards*. This explains that the cards belonged to the boys.
There is one exception. *Its* is used for possession and *it's* stands for *it is*.

bold   Letters or words can be written in bold print, which is darker than normal. It can help to highlight words for the reader.
For example: *'Promise me, you will **never** do that again.'*

brackets   Brackets can be used to add an extra comment, fact or aside into a sentence, e.g. *I am thirsty (who wouldn't be?) as a camel.*

capital letter   A capital letter starts the first word of a new sentence. It is a letter written in the upper case, e.g. JOIN NOW.

caption   A caption is a short sentence or phrase used with a picture.

classic poetry   This is poetry that has survived the test of time.

clause   A clause is a group of words that shows an event or situation. It contains a subject and a verb, e.g. *I ran*. In this clause, *I* is the subject and *ran* is the verb.

colon/ semi-colon   A colon is a punctuation mark (:) often used either:
1 To introduce a list in instructions, e.g. *You will need: two tyres, ...*
2 To add further information to a sentence, e.g. *I am quick at running: as fast as a cheetah.*
A semi-colon is a punctuation mark (;) that separates two main clauses, e.g. *I like cheese; it is delicious.*

comma	A comma is a punctuation mark (,) used to separate parts in a sentence. When reading you have to leave a pause when there is a comma. Commas can be used: 1 To separate items in a list, e.g. *a sunny day, a stretch of sand, a pile of good books, several rock pools and an ice-cream van.* 2 To separate pieces of information, e.g. *That's true, yes, that's true.* 3 When addressing someone by name, e.g. *I know, Wayne.* 4 After a subordinate clause which starts a sentence, e.g. *Although it is cold, I am warm.* 5 After many connecting adverbs used to start a sentence, e.g. *However, penguins can get cold…*
comparative	See **adjective**.
complex sentence	See **sentence**.
compound sentence	See **sentence**.
conjunction	A conjunction is a word used to link clauses within a sentence, e.g. *and, but, so, until, when, as,* e.g. *He had a book in his hand when he stood up.*
connective	A connective is a word or a phrase that links clauses or sentences. Connectives can be **conjunctions** (e.g. *but, when, because*) or connecting adverbs (e.g. *however, then, therefore*).
dash	A dash is a punctuation mark (–) often used in informal writing or in place of other punctuation marks, e.g. *It was fun – we all loved it.*
definition	A definition is an explanation of the meaning of a word. For example: **purse** a small bag for holding money.
dialogue	Dialogue is the term used to describe a conversation.
discussion writing	This type of text sets out both sides of an argument and draws a conclusion, supported by reasoning and evidence. Discussion texts set out to provide a balanced argument.
exclamation mark	An exclamation mark is a punctuation mark (!) used to end an exclamation, such as joy, anger, surprise, e.g. *Oh dear!*
explanation	This type of text explains a process: how or why things happen, e.g. *How a kite flies.* Explanations hinge around the word *because* as they are based on an explanation of 'cause' and 'effect'.
full stop	A full stop (.) is a punctuation mark used at the end of a sentence.
heading	A heading is a title that may be used to show the reader what a paragraph or section of text is about.
hyphen	A hyphen is a short dash used to join words together, e.g. *snake-pit*.
instruction	This text helps readers to make something or to carry out a sequential operation.
italic	Italic writing is a writing style that slopes. It can be used to help highlight words for the reader (e.g. *Charlotte's Web* by E.B. White)
noun	A noun is a word that names something or somebody. For example: *fox, chicken, brother, rock, sea, cloud, picture.* Nouns can be singular (*dog*) or plural (*dogs*). A collective noun refers to a group, e.g. a *flock* of birds. A proper noun begins with a capital letter and names something specifically, e.g. *Mrs Brown, London.*
passive	See **active**.

performance poetry	This is a form of poetry that can be performed aloud, often with music or a number of readers.
person (1st, 2nd or 3rd person)	1st person is used to talk about oneself – *I/we*. 2nd person is used to talk about whoever is listening or reading – *you*. 3rd person is used to refer to someone or somebody else – *he, she, it, they*. For example: *I* feel like *I've* been here for days. Look what *you* get, when *you* join the club. *He* says *it* takes real courage.
persuasive writing	This type of text intends to persuade the reader to a certain standpoint. Powerful language may be used with supporting arguments and evidence.
phrase	A phrase is a group of words that act as a unit. There are four types: 1 a noun phrase, e.g. *the beautiful, clever Siamese cat* 2 an adjectival phrase, e.g. *deep crimson* 3 an adverbial phrase, e.g. *very slowly* 4 a prepositional phrase, e.g. *at the end of the lane*.
playscript	A playscript is the written down version of a play and is used by actors.
plural	See **singular**.
preposition	A word that suggests the position of something by place (*on, in*) or direction (*over, beyond*) or time (*during, on Friday*).
pronoun	A pronoun is a word that can replace a noun. For example: *I, me, you, he, him, she, her, we, us, it, they, them, mine, yours, his, hers, ours, theirs, its, myself, herself, himself, themselves.*
poem	A poem is a text which creates or recreates experience in a compressed and intense way, using rhythm or rhyme and language effects to create images and sound effects.
punctuation	Punctuation is the term given to those marks used to help a reader, such as full stop (.), question mark (?), comma (,), exclamation mark (!), speech mark (' and '), colon (:) and semi-colon (;).
question mark	A question mark (?) is a punctuation mark that is used to end a question sentence. For example: *What part will you play?*
recount	This type of text tells the reader about what has happened, e.g. news, a diary.
report	This type of text provides information about a subject.
sentence	All sentences begin with a capital letter and end with a full stop, question mark or exclamation mark. A sentence must 'make sense', and be complete. There are four types: 1 *Statements* – that declare something and end in a full stop (.), e.g. *The class yelled in triumph.* 2 *Questions* – that ask something and end in a question mark (?). 3 *Exclamations* – that exclaim and end in an exclamation mark (!). 4 *Imperatives* – that command or instruct, with the verb near the start of the sentence, e.g. *Turn the knob.* Simple sentences are made up of one clause, e.g. *I am hungry.* Compound sentences are made up of two or more main clauses, joined by *and, but* or *so*, e.g. *I am hungry and I am thirsty.* Complex sentences are made up of one main clause and one, or more, subordinate clauses. A subordinate clause cannot stand on its own and relies on the main clause. It adds extra information, e.g. *I am thirsty because the well is dry.*

simile A simile creates a picture in the reader's mind by comparing one thing to another. There are two types: Some nights the moon is *like a banana*. Other nights it is *as round as a coin*.

singular/ plural Singular refers to one thing. Plural refers to more than one thing. For example:
dog (singular)   *sky* (singular)   *wolf* (singular)   *ditch* (singular)
dogs (plural)   *skies* (plural)   *wolves* (plural)   *ditches* (plural)

speech marks Speech marks (' and ') are punctuation marks that enclose speech, including the relevant sentence punctuation.
For example: *'What is it?' she gasped.*
In direct speech you write down what is said, e.g. *'Hello children,' said Tom.*
In indirect speech you report on what was said, e.g. *Tom said hello to the children.*

speech verbs Speech verbs are the verbs used before or after speech to show how the speech has been spoken. The most common is *said*. Others include *roared, whispered, chanted, muttered*.

standard English Standard English is the form of English used in most writing and by educated speakers. It can be spoken with any accent. There are many slight differences between standard English and local ways of speaking, e.g. *'We were robbed'* is standard English but in speech some people say, *'We was robbed.'*

story A story is a text type that recounts an invented tale. It is usually used to entertain. Stories normally have a setting and characters, and are structured by a plot.

sub-heading A sub-heading comes below a heading and indicates to the reader the contents of smaller units of text.

superlative See **adjective**.

tense A tense is a verb form that shows whether events happen in the past, present or the future. For example:
The Pyramids are on the west bank of the River Nile. (present tense)
They were built as enormous tombs. (past tense)
They will stand for centuries to come. (future tense)
Most verbs change their spelling by adding *ed* to make the past tense, e.g. *walk/walked*. Some have irregular spellings, e.g. *catch/caught*.

title A title is the overall heading given to a text.

verb A verb shows the action in a sentence and can express a process or state.
1 Verbs are often known as 'doing', 'being' or 'happening' words. For example, in the following sentence the word *run* is the verb.
The boys run down the hill.
2 Sometimes several words make up the verb. For instance: *The boys are running*. In this case *running* is the main verb and *are* is an extra verb that adds to the meaning. It is called an **auxiliary verb**.
3 Powerful verbs are vivid and expressive, e.g. *glare* instead of *look*.

viewpoint The viewpoint is the perspective from which a story is told, e.g. *I ran down the lane* (main character's viewpoint) or *She ran down the lane* (narrator's viewpoint).